Before the sun wakes up

Before the sun wakes up

Zainab Uddin

بسم الله الرحمن الرحيم

Contents

Moments and Musings

This poetry.
I never know what I'm going to say.
I don't plan it.
When I'm outside the saying of it, I get very
quiet and rarely speak at all.

- *Rumi*

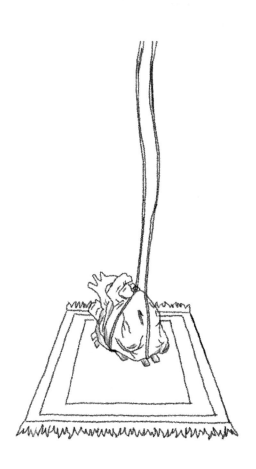

Fibs of Nightfall

Underneath the canopy of night,
I feel the distance turn me into a sand grain
displaced in the universe.
My soul crouches inside of me, hiding from
the beloved.
I fear I am too distant from my lord.

Scattered across the sky, tallies of the crimes
I have committed in the dark.
The stillness of night reveals the past that is
buried inside the walls of the hallowed
library built amongst the angels who perch
upon my shoulders –
Celestial scribes pouring out my secrets
back into my heart.

I am still standing there, gazing,
Spellbound by the starry expanse above me,
Leaning into the dark in an attempt to touch
the twinkling lights,
Trying to thieve a luminosity that could
perhaps drown the melancholy draped over
myself.

Woe to you night!

For you were a bystander watching me set
fire to myself.
Woe to you for not gifting me the dreams
you gave to Yusuf (a.s),
You carried his prophecy with reverence
And watched on him with adoration as he
fell into every trap but despair.

Woe to me for despair.
Will I lose the silver thread embroidered
into my fate because of the shadow of my
hubris that has turned me away?
I am trapped under this sky,
Like a fish inside of a bowl, I am contained,
unable to quench the thirst that swells in
your absence
and in my anticipation, I have become
smitten with the stars

Their light stirs a feeling inside me that
compels me to confess my hidden desires.
They pierce out the thread of shame that is
knotted inside my joints with a plaintive cry,

Moulding a false pretence of security, and
like a puppet on a string they dictate my
reality.
Naïve, we make a pact to remain united
evermore.
The fool in me swallows this lie.
Even as the beaming rays of the sun cast
shadows upon my grove.

You leave me, just as I reveal myself.

Woe to you night,
For tricking me with your lantern eyes,
For falling in love with the evening primrose
Who stays awake for you when I cannot.
Maybe we were not made to love.

I shatter the pedestal of you I sculpted with
my palms,
Just as Abraham did in Babylon.
I am overcome by the scorching heat from
the sun,
And I envy the coolness God bestowed upon
him.

I unload the burdens from my shoulders and
place them between my fingertips,
Raising them to the sky,
Calling onto my beloved
Who is above the canopy of night.

A dagger to faith

I stole a mad flame from you,
A wicked light you borrowed from the devil.
It was your refuge; my radiance
Turned pale with your cruel orbit.
You killed the morning and left me in
mourning,
Melodies disrupted by the dreamers
yearning.
I was the dreamer once, in love with the
heavens and the moon,
That lump of rock that lingers in space
It must be the same one Ahmed (ﷺ)
looked onto.
He swallowed divine secrets,
Brimmed with dew drop tears wondering
about this darkness I have consumed.
The skies sent down holy water from the
heavens, with the command of my beloved,
to extinguish this flame.

The shadows stayed quiet,
watching through the surface.
They do not encourage, nor oppose.

The shadows refuse to speak so long as I am
radiant.
Your wretched curses I have buried inside
life's casket,
Mouldering inside frigid tombs.
Bad company fish for the light inside you,
An unquenched thirst, a dagger to faith,
The shadow that spoke
Hangs on a stake

Bird

Like a bird inside an aviary,
I am somewhere I do not recognise.
Stuck in the middle of a noisy street,
Sounds I can hear, but what do they mean?
I am dumb when it comes to translating this
in the way you intended for me.

Secret

The only secret I know how to keep is the
one I make with you.
Only then does my tongue obey your rules.
What would people say if they knew what
you do?
If they could witness all the darkness I have
consumed,
Would they stand still as my soul trembles
in fear of losing you?
How long can I hide before the trumpet
shatters the truth?
How long before this curtain is removed?
Would it have been enough that I confessed
it all to you?

Chasing the Robin

My caravan halted on the narrow, winding
road,
caught in a moment of reverie.
Inside this sanctuary stood a sprawling
labyrinth, leaking with memories I detained,
every artifact a doorway to another.
Exploring this whimsical wonderland,
I greet old friends, now adorned as glass
figurines,
a treasured keepsake I bury inside of this
van.
Broken ties, like the frayed strands of silk
that remain from the wounded web the
spider once built.

Severed bridges—
a gaping chasm between two souls who
would once rush to greet one another, now
do not look,
with churning currents of water still gushing
below them,
both now refuse to endure the cold winds to
meet,
when in former years the storms could not
keep them afoot

It is better to leave than to love,
the shadows speak.

Perhaps every love is futile in this life,
A temporary world full on provisional love.
Why then does the pain refuse to abate?
How will I raise my flag of truce
when a part of me is still sanguine like
Prophet Yaqub (upon whom be peace),
whose vision returned with the fragrance of
Yusuf?
Will old friends return too?

Walls of the caravan press in on me like a
vise,
memories cling like second skin.
I fumble with the lock and turn the latch to
release,
drinking the air like a camel empties an
oasis.
The world is alive with symphony and allure
trepidation washes over the crowded streets
as lights flash and flicker, teasing me.
My instinct is to indulge, but I turn away
quietly.

It has become a habit to search for comfort
in the colours of the sky,
pour out my uncertainty to the clouds who
grow sombre with sin just as the stone once
did –
the silence is punctured by the gentle rustle
of leaves as the robin weaves a path through
busy streets.
Light and shadow flicker over me,
my wings are clipped and I am unable to
soar the heights I once knew.
I am tethered to the ground whilst the robin
flutters away
Where does it go?
Does it return to heaven?

Will the chance ever come to hear the gentle
lapping of water against the shore,
angels chanting, hymning melodies
in praise of my Lord?
Will the chance ever come?
The only palace I built was on hidden hopes
and straws.
Will the chance ever come

when the only pain I have can be contained
inside of a van,
when there are infant soldiers chocking
inside the folds of earth being pushed on by
man,
when they are bleeding with blood and me
with water and salt?
I return back to pick up the threads of my
journey once more,
My soul is wrapped in a shroud of guilt.
In a flash I careen off the road, and plunge
into a dark abyss.
Memories fling out like debris after a storm,
Glass figurines all bleed onto the floor
As the earth welcomes my dead corpse.

My caravan remains anchored to the ground
but I rise to the sky,
following the robin back into paradise

Farwell oh caravan, I held you close,
but you were just a vehicle to return me
back home.

Before the sun

How can I doubt
the prayers you wake me up for
before the sun?
I must be wishing for something
you can't wait to pass on.

Hope

Allah's kindness colours the sky.
Never despair, for his mercy weighs down
the clouds,
and with every splatter of rain He sends your
way,
He is rinsing you of your past mistakes,
Preparing you for a greater fate.

Excuses

My mind is filled with questions I do not
ask,
because I'm convinced the answer was told
to everyone else.
How do I formulate my speech from
thoughts I am afraid to say out loud?
When did I miss out?
I cannot enter that day with these empty
excuses I have printed out on this page.
I must start searching now.
History only proves time cannot be
contained.

Fallen Planets

Inside the jar of my heart,
I carry the past that is still warm,
filled with seething wounds,
shreds of myself muddied by former friends,
a butterfly caught in a spider's web,
its wings now tattered, its colour dead.

My voice trembles at dawn,
The past lunges at me whispering cold
despair,
Memories echo,
The powerless plea,
I talk to God of ghosts that still haunt me.

Held captive by fickle nostalgia,
A drunken dance,
Shadows congregate to shed in the dark.

Planets fall onto my lap,
I fear the worlds will collapse if I stand,
I learn to sit, perform patience, lift up my
hands,
Sacred prayers leave my mouth,
My Lord carries His planets back.

Decimated worries bleed from dismal eyes,
Once a home for sorrow, now invites grace
inside.

Cheap Love

Moments of sadness
and disappointment creep in
as you try to find yourself in
people and not Him.
To give a person this much of you
is to guarantee yourself a void,
digging a pit inside you,
waiting for it to be filled with what
people could never afford.

Missing God

Love cannot stay hidden.
It spills out in every form.
This love you sprouted in me before I was
born,
I only wish the yearning could be as loud as
the day I entered this world.
How can a child overtake me in my faith?
How can I live up to my past-self and return
back to the child missing God again?

Ceiling

On the nights where my soul does not want
to leave,
I wonder how much I truly know about
myself.
If I take away all the influences that I am
wrapped inside,
will I find that I am as blank as the ceiling I
gaze at night?
Strange, I realise every celling carries a
light,
And I recognise that within me,
Faith harbours mine.

Muddy

The doorman of my heart is naïve and kind,
inviting fugitives inside.
Strangers who crouch behind masks,
a buried treasure I am greedy to unwrap.
Drift into the distance,
I'll too sit with you in the mud,
shared consciousness cannot go untouched.
Drift into the distance,
I am alone now in the mud,
I was a friend to solace long before we met.
God will send down rain to caress my tear
drops.
Drift into the distance,
forgiveness has found out.
Oh, if it was as simple
For my dislike to despise you,
Perhaps I would have been alright.
But your luck transcends time.
The doorman of my heart still watches over
the past.

Flawed

A solemn soul clings to wilting dreams,
painted melancholy stained on the believers'
fingertips,
thirsty for distant dreams.
Grim spectres watch upon my barren heath,
buried hopes smothered by water and clay.
Bid farewell to future days,
before the heavens greet me, I must silence
this rage.
A raucous noise,
my loudest flaw- tears kiss the floor.
The youth fleet with their complaints,
smothered by secrets,
tortured faith.
Will heaven greet the bruised one who falls
back on his mistake?
A solemn soul dreams still today.

Name

Faith dissipated into a noun,
a name we gave to distinguish ourselves.
Later, we cracked open the vowels
And rinsed out every trace of
The character it once held.

Sin

Tears, a shuddering breath and a promise I
make,
and in that moment even as you can see the
entire scope of my life, and the promise I
will betray over and over again,
you forgive me anyways.
Your mercy can not be contained; it runs
wild, chasing to greet the souls who you
decreed would capture an emotion so
beloved to you-
regret you planted inside the sinner who
tries, an excuse for you to forgive all the
time.

But every transgression left a mark,
remnants of sin clouding my heart,
and so, my vision is blurred, and I am afraid,
with the devil whispering this time you
won't forgive me again,
and I eat his lies like I've been starved a
fortnight.
The side effects of my sin,
drooping veils in front of my eyes,
making it easier for me to be swayed to
every side.

Good deeds

Everyone one of us is a parent,
Breathing life into our deeds,
and just as the parent raises their child with
the unspoken rule;
to swap the duty of care when the wrinkles
start to appear,
the deeds we produce are formulated the
same,
Only they will transcend realms to look after
you in the grave.

Friend-ship

We sing our song to summers dream,
Sprinkling dew splatters into springs.
You shelter me from cruel storms that have
withered me.
Portals inside conversations,
Reminiscent with you,
Frosty past turns warm.
I still grieve the thieves I once knew.
Behind the fog,
We set forth to the sea,
Inside a friend-ship,
You see me.
We harvest new thoughts,
Fertile dreams begin to bloom.
Your luminescent perfume lingers
throughout the day.
The moon stays awake to ask me about
what we did today.

Intertwined

You made me believe the worst version of
myself was still alive.
I doused those demons with gasoline long
before our paths intertwined,
but you summoned them back to life.
You resurrected my past and used me as a
weapon against myself.
I can hear the words aloud,
Vibrations mimicking the rhythm of my
heart.
You opened up the same wound you helped
treat,
Leeching off my scars.
I gifted you my trust and every good thought
I could find.
You gifted me back
The worst version of myself.

Dream

In my sleep you bury my thoughts,
Opening up the doors of this cage
and I wander out searching for something I
cannot explain.
My eyes are shut yet I see more than when I
am awake,
experiences I taste without a tease of it in
the day.
Ecstasies are different inside of this realm,
I do not know what any of it could mean,
but it tastes like a sip of something I already
have inside of me.
I recognise your touch in this,

my soul remembers its origins.

The rules of loving

I've come to the conclusion
Finally,
that you only make people
I love disappoint me
to remind me how fragile
this love can be.
You send these lessons to me,
teaching me to turn to you completely.
I often give myself away too quickly,
trying to please people to
keep them around me.
I get lost in loving completely,
with a love that has no capacity to
carry anymore of this world inside me.

You taught me the rules of loving too,
I should never love a person
in the same way I love you.
I never realised how dangerous loving could
be,
until I watched so many leave.

Polished Moments

Turn to me.
Reveal the goodbye you snatched from the
sparrow's beak.
Swallows, hawks and eagles all leave.
You took to the winds and left me with the
coming of spring,
the autumnal leaves rustling mournfully in
your wake.
How do I grieve the passing of someone
whose heart still beats?

Merry peals of children's laughter and
giggles ring,
the sun is smiling.
Golden halos glisten, cast above the
innocent.
Hearts like light bulbs beam, flickering in
sync.
Let them bask in joy while trees are still
budding.
Let them, let them, let them scream.

I have been quiet for long,
plasters taped over my lips, stifling the
words that once flowed so freely.

I am afraid I resemble the hurricanes.
My words striking with the force of a
sudden storm.
I shout and rage, yet, in truth, I am no real
threat,
merely a child's tantrum, longing to be heard
by those who only listen when there is
commotion.
Let me, let me, let me speak

Adults smile under the moonlight,
reminiscing on moments they've polished.
Aware of their deceit, but they seem content
with dishonesty,
seeking to retrieve lightbulbs dimmed by
winters wind.
Let them, let them, let them believe

Your new life, I wondered about it.
Do you know the merry children of
yesterday grew into wistful adults today?
I, too, have learned to take flight and soar
through the streets, just like you once did.
You left in silence, and for a time, I hated
the quiet,

but I have lifted that bandage.
Oh, how I wish to tell you,
I don't hate you, not even a little bit.

This was Gods' kindness
I chased a world that did not want me.
Now, my heart soars towards My beloved.
Lord, teach me the ways of love anew.
Let me scream, let me speak, let me believe,
I turn to you
Let me, please.

A Message in a Bottle

I throw my complaints into the ocean,
a message inside of a bottle.
A secret shrouded in glass,
banished from the curse of human hands.

Will the churning waves shatter my vial,
scattering fragments of shards into the
ocean,
ripples of my past mistake assaulting calm
waters,
or will the gentle waves cradle my message
with the same tenderness
they caressed Moses?

O dwellers of the ocean,
Grant me the same clemency you granted
Younes (a.s)
Guard my message and do not mock me.
My strength is waning,
I fear I may lose my grip too soon,
forgive me for disturbing you.

I plunge into the blue expanse,
panic seized,
limbs flounder, frantic, flail

51

I curse the ocean for its treachery,
the perilous game it chose to play with me.

Thrashing in fury at the sea's cruel face,
I missed the grace in the waves' embrace.
The ocean too had taken pity on me,
the very force I cursed,
Had rescued me.

I longed to sink beneath the waves,
why then did I fight to stay awake?
Perhaps I wanted to kill something inside of
me,
not myself, not really.

Amidst panic, the bottle emerged from the
sea,
Weathered and frosted,
it lay washed up next to me.
With trembling hands, I pried the cork from
its neck,
unravelling a tightly wound message.
A golden inscription, an answer to cope,
Good deeds to wipe off old woes.

*"He who repents and renews their faith
and starts to do good deed to wipe of bad
deeds for those people Allah will exchange
their past sins into good deeds,
and your lord is ever so forgiving most
merciful."*

(25:70)

House of Straws

I am a tenant inside a house of straws,
built on thin woven wishes that shatter under
winters claw.
Besieged—
wolves lurking on prowl biding their time,
glinting with the promise of impending
doom,
waiting to pounce on my latent dreams,
tattered remains in the wake of
harbingers of my own wound.

Quivering hands, like autumn leaves,
lay to rest dreams never given a chance to
bloom,
snatched in the shadows,
breaths stolen,
akin to the fate of Abel's emblem.
A solemn burial, a dirge for what could have
been,
quivering hands tremble in their own sin.

Was it not the brothers of Yusuf (a.s) who
murdered a sheep,
rinsing their sins with purloined bleeding?

Did this ram rise to martyrdom before me?
Will my dreams be welcomed into paradise
with scorn and laughter,
taunting the killer, I am becoming?
Trapped inside the labyrinth of regret for the
paths not taken,
I've forfeited everything.

My house of straws crumbles beneath the
scorching heat,
A merciless foe melting away the fortress
that had imprisoned me.
I once preferred you, O' sun, over the moon,
but now your beaming rays seem to taunt
me.
Which direction do I take,
for I have long forgotten life outside of my
straw house?

I remember many moons ago,
when my dreams were the spark that kindled
my soul,
but even then, there were flaws in my zeal.
I would become elated at the seed of the
thought,

I was hazy with smoke before I could begin.
A barren mind with empty spots awaiting
the arrival of trees.

The sun spills out her rays,
golden threads woven into the horizon.
Perhaps it was foolish of me to blame,
with the sun's gentle touch, I can see the
world today.
Why do I fret for tomorrow when destinies
are written?
When portents have appeared before me,
illuminating the path I must take.
I forgive you, sun.
Forgive me.

My dreams; human ash,
Scattered across valleys of the pious.

*My child keep your dreams far from your
heart,
hold every feeling between your fingers and
raise them to God.
Only he can teach you the language of
wolves,*

*only he can imbue you with the wisdom to
lead,
only the Divine can summon the winds to
sweep away your uncertainty.
The rays of sun should only beam on your
face,
your soul should not be moved by
compliments.
A house of straw will always break,
why drown in sorrow over fate?
Why succumb to shadows when the beloved
awaits?*

Passed away

I can't write words
Profound enough to honour you,
So why try to
when tears can decipher
my thoughts
more accurately
then words could ever have
The power to?

Distant Rage

I draw the curtains of this ancient tale.
The victim is a corpse of memories,
flung from his passionate love; the life
behind him.
Lines of poetry blur with age.
A friend turns foe too quickly.
How to hate the one to whom your soul once
confided?
Wipe the colour off your eyes,
tell the heart to be quiet.
Footsteps lead to the evening's cave,
solace for the tired.
Distant rage,
flames mellowed by tear droplets,
the body mourns beside an empty grave.
Grief to grudge is the wrong way.
Why stretch this heart for hate?

Burnt

Hearts softened by hot pain,
cauterized to silence.
Festering wounds carry bad omens.
No sound. Cries, no sound.
Thoughts rebel seething with violence.
Holes inside the curses,
prisoners of the lord carry his remembrance.
"Let the fire be cool," the pain listens.
Every labouring thought is slaughtered.
A sacrificed wound,
Sleep resumed
Delusions at dawn charming the slaves
amongst you.
Prisoners rebel when disaster strikes.
Playing with flames,
Weeping through the night,
Can the burnt one still enter paradise?

Twice

I haven't forgotten you.
I've been hiding you in my heart.
Maybe that's selfish,
burying you twice,
but how else to get on with life?

After Dark

There was a feeling that sat in my heart after
the dark.
My bones bickering over verbs that stayed
nouns,
loosening the latch that kept my rib cage
locked.
I was both dispersed and exposed at the
same time.
The putrid scent of your goodbye left a bitter
taste in my mouth.
It lingered longer than our timeline.

I swallowed my truth - veracity was an
oversaturated sport that reeked both
exhaustion and ridicule.
I would be left with repercussions of my
speech.
I would say the wrong words and spend a
million days visiting every other door I
could've opened instead of the ones I did.
I'll stay quiet because I don't want to be
alone with the sensations running in my
skin, pacing down every thought,
teasing me with an insecurity that
heightened as you walked away,
maybe some part of me isn't enough.

I latched onto this goodbye you baked.
I tasted every ingredient and then threw it up
again.
I poisoned myself with your concoction of a
truth that expired long before it was made.
The pain now is the only proof I have left of
this friendship we sent to the grave.

Beautiful enemy

I don't know when I taught myself
how to think,
and how miserably I failed at learning it.
Creating worries from every blessing,
I have realised I find flaws in everything.
Beauty terrifies me, because
my eyes are more gullible than me,
and I fear when I'm hungry,
I will befriend a beautiful enemy.

Continued

My soul recognises yours.
This isn't our first meeting,
can you recall the moments we shared
before we followed Adam or
did the distance separate us two?
Do you remember me?
You must do,
because your soul didn't greet mine,
They just continued

Buried out back

Flickering lights,
Witnesses dissolved into the abyss of time.
Injustices bouncing inside my mind, teasing every crime you committed against me,
a threat, a letter so dark I was enslaved by the words you did not write.
I was slipping on every memory that spilt out of my mind and landed in front of me,
a television series starring me.
I craved night, but it too turned against me, torturing me, breathing life into remains of souvenirs I collected of our time.
I was locked out.
My eyes trying to drift to sleep only to meet you in my dreams,
I tried to thieve peace but I got caught.

Already a criminal, I thought it was time.
With finicky hands, I buried you in the dark.
Maybe it was a fissure between mates that turned us into the most wicked versions of ourselves,
but I could not ignore the delicacy that teased me as we became strangers again.
I buried you deeper than anyone else.
I let myself rest.

Was it selfish to choose me in the presence
of your memory,
 or was it the only way to free myself?
I could not digest the guilt flavoured of you.
I was wrong to think I escaped.
A fortnight passed and you confirmed my
doubts were true.
Your clammy skin and darting eyes met
with mine as you whispered,
"I will not leave until you give me what I
want."
I knew you would come back to haunt me
for this,
a piece of the puzzle only I can gift.

Forgiveness you sought out,
And I gave it to you.
Pieces of myself I collected,
some I threw,
but I put myself back together
just like I always do.

I'll be quiet too

If silence is how you
console yourself,
then I'll be quiet too,
even if the silence is
deafening me with worry for you.
Silence is all you've known,
I'll practice it with you.
I'll teach my eyes to speak
Softer than my words do.
I like you too much
to start missing you
too.

Mother Tongue

I was not raised by gentle women,
grit in her voice,
broken English used to fix domestic wars.
Ancient hands used to stitch the fabric of
love she collected from her mother, and her
mother before her.
Blood dampening through the sheets,
passing down the pain she swallowed when
she couldn't speak.
Her mother tongue was alive,
it was sharp,
but time wasn't her ally and soon her womb
would stretch for love only to carry a child
who would mimic the new sounds she didn't
yet understand,
and the laughter she heard from strangers
would leak into her house.
She would practice traditions,
resurrecting her ancestors every time she felt
alone,
asking to grease my hair met with a "No!"
She would feed a village with one hand,
her feet would make concrete collapse.
Timestamps marking her body where the
pain resides.

Residues of love spilling into every remark,
hospitality she decorated day and night,
because as strong she was,
The little girl inside her
just wanted to be liked.

Hufu

Inside paradise, my auntie will smile
without carrying the weight of worry etched
upon her by fear
of losing moments too quickly.
Love slipping through time,
leasing this body that is prone to breaking
itself.
Shattered glass, pain scattered, aching ache
throbbing where the heart resides.

She is the daylight,
yearning for a fierce meeting with the deep
night,
waiting for the sun to hide,
Eager to pour forth the fog that has brewed
within her mind.
No longer concealed, her emotions cease
their disguise.
Everybody carries something that keeps
them up at night.

Inside paradise, my auntie will smile,
And I will too,
Our spirits intertwined.
Maybe we will visit Ayyub (pbuh),

and she will reminisce on this world and all
of it abuse.
Pain will retreat, and a tender smile will
bloom,
ethereal gleam awaits you.

Everything will be alright Hufu,
inside of this sacred realm,
love reclaims its smile's domain.

The Tree and Me

A cluster of kids gather by its trunk,
beams of sunshine peek through the gnarled
branches,
caressing the small hands and feet that
embrace her friend, the tree.

From the moment we met,
I sensed it was a special meeting.
It seems I do that often,
overestimate a person, make them my
friend.
Now, as I stand here beside this magnificent
tree,
I wonder which branch you took when you
left me.
If it brings you joy, then I will plant one for
you in its place,
but leave mine be, for too many have stolen
many from me.

It is as if I have become a child once more,
except then, I was brave,
letting others hear my pain.
But now an adult, I have become wise,

only letting the heavens hear me weep to
God.

Under this pressure, I fear I may crack.
I envy the ones who have turned to
diamonds beneath this weight,
while I remain a mere lump of coal,
wondering if I have strayed from the path I
was meant to walk.
I am crippled by the fear of disappointing
my Lord,
as if my efforts fall short, and my devotion
is flawed.
What if my actions are not enough?
Will he take away that which I hold close?
It's a selfish thought, I know.
Perhaps I deserve to be left alone.
How do I continue to disappoint the only
one who does not make me feel like I am
difficult to adore?

I glance back at this tree,
undaunted by the rough assault of children
with their hands and feet,
whilst syllables are enough to ruin me.

Perhaps I should become its students and let
it teach,
for in the stillness of nature, true answers are
reached.

One child reaches the pinnacle
she gazes down with a grin,
seemingly conquering the world beneath.
In her elation, she falters, her grip slips,
and with a jarring crack, she plummets.
Perhaps this is how the Almighty looks onto
me,
so enraptured by my own success,
I neglect the very foundations that buoyed
me.
I stumble and crash, only then realizing my
folly.

The child survives with a broken leg.
I continue my life with a limp and
recovering faith.

Dad

Every time I was sure I couldn't do
something,
you convinced me I could.
Your words, I play in my head,
over and over again,
carvings on wood.
You are the reason I could do everything
I was afraid of.
You held me the right way,
resting my head on your lap as you prayed
is my favourite memory of being eight .
My protection always,
My dad,
The biggest believer in our house.

Too soon

I watched you leave.
I stood in your room,
whispering prayers for you to hear.
It was morning still,
but night filled the room.
You left too early,
the morning was too soon.

Paper thin

This paper was thin, but it carried a
wreckage of leaden words that my body
could no longer contain.

This paper was strong,
It maintained its composure even after I
confessed to it your every sin,
remnants of you I spilt – a boneyard of
bodies I scattered across the page,
but she handled you with the delicacy of
grace.

This paper was friendly,
she listened to my soliloquy of shame,
reaching out to unload every baggage of you
I kept both on purpose and by mistake,
holding on until the karmic scales fell into
place.

This paper was a gift to myself I gave,
in an attempt to pull out the words you
sowed – like apples of a tree they flourished
where they belonged, and I never missed a
day of watering,
I helped it grow.

This paper is different to every other one I
have met.
She reads me even before I reach out for my
pen.

This paper is a thief who stole you from me,
pierced you out from inside,
spillages of ink bleeding out,
Staining my hands.

This paper was my final goodbye.
A cremation of a thousand memories in my
mind,
A blaze of fireworks colouring the sky,
You left as you came the first time,
An explosion of colour blinding my eyes.

Healing

I think I'm finally healing,
maybe pouring little parts of myself to
someone else
Isn't losing.
Maybe,
it's finally breathing.

Habit

It has become a habit
to prepare myself for the worst,
to live inside a nightmare
I can plot in my head.
It is a dangerous habit
to be so full-on breadcrumbs of love.
It is a habit I must break before
I sell myself.

Blue

You left with a cliff-hanger,
For so long I tried to reach you.
Now I sit on this cliff and
envy the view,
watching the waves wash out
every shade of blue.

A whisper of peace

Praying and still feeling confused,
How do I know if this is good for me?
I pray to you for clarity,
I'm yet to receive any.
Often, I doubt everything I have worked
towards,
guarding myself with worries, doubting the
prayers I read,
What if I'm praying for something that isn't
written for me?
If only I could meet future me,
Maybe it would be easier to hope if I could
catch a glimpse of when hope listens to me.
What if I'm wasting my prayers, and
sacrificing sleep, asking for something
I will never receive?

I turn to you,
You grant tranquillity.
Maybe you're preparing me for something
better to receive,
maybe patience is what you're offering me.

Hypocrisy

I often find myself disregarding acts of piety
because of an insecurity that was planted
inside me:
Echoes of hypocrisy chanting the
inconsistencies in my sincerity.
I know I am not perfect,
the distance from me to it would be a
pathway that would take all of eternity.
I feel like an imposter when I practice my
faith in front of eyes,
even with my best intentions doubts flutter
in my mind,
and with fear of falling into hypocrisy,
I stop the very act you prescribed.
Foolish I am –
blindly wandering inside this trap,
letting a whisper of his
stop me from pleasing you, oh God.

Light

You didn't leave just as quickly as you
came.
Maybe if you had, it would've been easier to
pull myself together over your inevitable
fate.
Instead, I sunk into my skin in attempt to
escape this reality which would settle in
your name.

I was not ready,
I am not ready,
a million years on earth would have never
prepared me for the feelings that you gave
birth to as you passed away.
I didn't realise how much your love weighed
until it dissipated into a million tears on my
face.

In this moment, I want to forget you
In this moment, I want to capture everything
about you.
Grief settled in my throat,
Welded inside me.
My eyes, I stole from you, stayed soft,
So, I let them speak every memory of you
that I could not.

Before the Sun Wakes Up

Empty House

She finally realised:
Thieves don't go raiding an empty house.
That within her was a special kind of power,
A universe yet to reveal itself.

Mum and Dad

With all the love you gifted me,
was there enough left of it for you?
The child is hungry, thirsty, and scared of
this world.
A dream is burst open;
lights flicker as the years run away.
How did you always know the right words
to say?
Your wings are heavier now since I came.
Before me, did you fly,
soar through life?
Did I tether you to the ground?
Do you like this house or do you prefer the
clouds?
Words unsaid gather with dust,
a bookshelf of memories out of touch.
I am swallowed by fear—
the lighthouse is dim from here.
Your gentle voice puts my heart to sleep.
I always loved to stay awake,
to fit more of you inside my day.
Sometimes I wish I could walk to the past
and

greet this boy and girl before they become
mum and dad.
I won't tell them my name;
I'll just watch how they smile
and hope mum and dad are happier in life
with me inside.

Before I'm gone

Before I'm gone tell them that:
I was drunk on life.
Tell them I was a woman and a child all at
once.
Tell them my hobbies include rewriting
memories in my spare time.
Tell them I felt everything.
A thousand constellations creating identities
for personas to hide,
but I could see everything from looking into
your eyes.
Tell them I rub salt on my wounds.
Tell them I am never going to show how
much it hurt because, before I am flesh, I am
afraid.
Tell them I was scared.
Tell them I was a coward when it came to
losing,
so, I ended a million moments of greatness
before they could find me.
Tell them I was gullible.
Naïve was my excuse for trusting too
quickly.
Tell them I never forgot.
Tell them I was an artist

who tried to pause time through her brush
strokes.
Tell them I failed.
Tell them I prayed,
Hiding my sorrow into every crevice of my
faith,
whispering to my mat every worry that had
kept me awake.
Tell them I was lost,
Tell them I found my way back home again.

Moments and Musings

"The little things? The little moments? They aren't little."

— Jon Kabat-Zinn

Healthy remorse, Unhealthy shame

The deep-rooted consequences of shame lead to internalised suppression and thereafter a negative self-talk which grows and perpetuates into a cycle of abuse. Shaytan feeds shame and Allah feeds hope, the consequences of shame lead us to become hesitant towards Allah believing we are not worth his forgiveness, and are hypocrites when in factuality this is a complete allusion made to distract you from the fact that you are trying. Having low self-worth is a barrier to healing, and unresolved trauma will only grow into hatred for the self and for others around you.

The 'Saviour mentality' is a self-destructive approach to living. Many of us are 'problem solvers' but the issue here is you need to be looking for a problem to then be able to solve them; a double-edged sword - with a focus on problems you are only bound to stay unhappy and in a state of constant anxiety.

Often times we forget to be grateful and practice gratitude - if you are thankful, I will increase you' this works for both Allah and people because to fully appreciate a person is to motivate them. Shifting your focus to the blessings you have as oppose to problems will have a hugely positive impact to your life, this does not mean to suppress or hide emotion because to heal is to accept, and the fastest way out of a negative feeling is through it. Active action must be made and not a misunderstanding of a passive idea of 'sabr'.

Being sad does not contradict having patience, but what does is having resentment for Allah for what is happening. Changing the way you respond to pain, reduces pain- We must embody self-compassion in order to move forward- changing your understanding of who Allah is and having a positive perception of him will only aid you 'I am as my servant sees me' how are we seeing God?

Disappointment

People disappoint. No matter how much of yourself you give or how much you connected, how much of yourself you shared, love you borrowed, moulded and gifted - people will take advantage, sometimes the most painful ones are the ones unintended, the ones that happen in a flicker because you're a thought that got forgotten, a thing so easily expendable, a someone easy to make understand because you've decorated and daydreamed every excuse possible because how can someone I love make me feel so dispensable.

Maybe I have a habit of daydreaming, expecting the expectations I place on myself on other people, maybe not everyone cares, maybe caring is why it hurts. Maybe the love I give will always carry some sting - because I was convinced to find solace and peace in people and not Him.

Maybe people were made to disappoint as a calling, a turning to the only one who will exceed the expectations and yearning, who

will never need me to daydream an excuse
or reason, who will show me that people
who disappoint are people.

Just, people.

Not Him.

Endings

I guess there's a beauty to endings, a sort of hope and gratitude for the love we experienced because of how much it hurts. Maybe endings are what keeps us going, the inevitable end is the reason we cherish moments, the reason we savour the taste of a laugh, the feeling of a smile, the flicker in our hearts, maybe the ending is why we feel.

Sometimes I imagine a world without endings, how distant and beautiful it seems but I wonder how ugly and cruel that reality is; a curse, the ability to always have, to always continue, to not be able to cherish moments, memories, days, people, books, sunsets.

Healing

Maybe healing is so hard because it is so strongly reliant on hope, something we lose touch of as we get older and see how nasty and ugly the world can be, and the more heartbreak we witness in and around us sticks with us and hope is just a word, but I guess to believe that what's written for you will come, you need to believe everything happens for a greater purpose, and that it doesn't mean looking back at the ugly times through rose coloured glasses for the pain you endured, because you didn't deserve that hurt and convincing yourself you did won't heal you.

I wish I could take away all the pain you experienced, but the time you spent with yourself learning, caring, healing and building who you are, that is something I wish you never trade because you may not have deserved that pain, but you deserved to know that your soul is more powerful than you know, and that you are your greatest rainbow.

They call it the present because it's a gift

Maybe it's not one thing, maybe it's everything - maybe this is the best parts that we'll look back on, the memories we'll envy, the times we'll yearn, moments we'Il crave. Maybe there's a sadness to every happy memory, a ghost, a little reminder that we can never go back to moments that passed just as quickly as they came. Maybe we gloss our memories too much, looking at them through rose coloured glasses, forgetting the fights and shouts and silence, but we forget because maybe they're just not that important. The moments I'm living through now aren't perfect, but why let that stop me from creating beautiful memories, and stories I can hear my future self already sharing.

Your best

"Try your best" Your best isn't linear. Your best changes every day, some days the hardest thing to do is smile and other days laughter is easier. You're allowed to feel sad and bothered and stressed, allowed to feel lost in this great big space, allowed to mess up and make mistakes and not know how to say what you want to say, to forgive and try, because trying is proof of living. It's progress not perfect. it's a flawed attempt, it's an uncomfortable situation, it's effort. And effort is a dare, it's a risk worth taking. There's a beauty in the effort, souls recognise purity and the best efforts are made with sincerity so effort is never wasted, it's experienced. It's okay if your best today was just smiling, not just, it's okay if your best today was smiling, at least you're trying.

Forgiveness

Forgiveness is not accepting or forgetting the moments that tested you, or surrendering to the hurt they've caused you. Forgiveness is giving yourself the peace you need to get through. It is exhausting yourself of all the pain, and healing the parts of you that should have never been torn. Forgiveness is not linear and some days it's harder to look at them with clarity. Some days it's closer to easy, sometimes we trade forgiveness with time and that's why an adult can live with the wounds of their inner child. Forgiving is beautiful, but for someone who has already poured out so much of themselves forgiving isn't always a way out.

Slipping up

Slipping up doesn't mean you've failed, it doesn't diminish everything you've done up until this moment, it doesn't take away the battle you fought up, sometimes a step back is needed to remind you of how far you've come, to teach you that you left certain habits for a reason, to remind you that you are capable, that you've done this once, that learning takes time and mastering takes more, and those little bumps on the road are reminders to slow down, to check in on yourself, to take care of you, because it doesn't matter how many times you fall, it matters how many times you try, and falling only gives reasons to stand, so stand. And don't fear the fall, it only teaches you everything you'd have missed standing.

Poking Hearts

Sometimes the people who are doing the poking are the same ones who are hurting. Every word has its own flavour, some words seem sweet, some are laced with conceit, some sound like laughs but if you look close enough you can almost taste the salt, the yearning, the empty, the thirst of that person trying so hard not to dream, because maybe every dream they've ever had was ruined, every happy ending was a lie and they can't help but feel a poke in their heart when you have everything they can't let themselves dream about. Too often the pokes in our hearts lead us to point our fingers, to blame and hurt others but I think I'm coming to realise that even a poke in the heart is a touch, and we only hurt because we love, and maybe without the expectations our greatest enemy is just a person trying to cope.

Destiny

Destiny is a sort of reality we tend to forget. everything happens for a reason, but not every reason is reason enough, not every failure is a leap of faith or hope and not every happening is happy. We live in the dark for most of our lives in respective of our lives and it's scary to think how much we don't know about our life, and about ourselves- so how can we trust in making the right choices and decisions for ourselves? We can't - and in some way that's the purpose of destiny, a reassurance that the you will be where you are meant to be that you may not know your whole self but Allah does. You don't need to have the entire scope of your life decided for a you, you don't even know yet, live with the moments that come, meet the person you'll become, having a plan doesn't mean following a line, create your own, make turns - and know dead ends are only chances of a new beginning. Failure isn't a reality, it's a perception.

ACKNOWLEDGMENTS

To my beloved parents,

My heart overflows with gratitude for all that
you have done for me. From the earliest days of
my life, you nurtured my spirit, instilled in me
the values of Islam, and showed me the beauty
of love, compassion, and faith. Your unwavering
support, encouragement, and love have been the
foundation of my life, and I could not have
become the person I am today without you. I
dedicate this book to you with all my heart, as a
token of my love and appreciation.

To the 'Original Eight' - Faatima, Anisa, Abida,
Hamida, Sumayah, Maria, and Hibah

Words cannot express the depth of my love and
gratitude for each one of you. You have been my
companions, my confidantes, and my heart's
truest home. Your unwavering support, your
boundless love, and your unbreakable spirit have
inspired me to be the best version of myself, and
I am honoured to call you, my family.

To Marium

Thank you for showing me the brighter colours in life, for making me laugh the hardest and showing me what true friendship looks like.

To my adorable little ones,

Medina, Hannah, Humayrah, Safiyya, Sofia, Zacki, Zayd, Musa, and all the other wonderful kids in our big, joyful family. You fill my world with giggles, wonder, and endless smiles.

I love you all dearly.

Notes

Notes

Notes

Printed in Great Britain
by Amazon

29910025R00088